Vo Trong Nghia

Vo Trong Nghia / Building Nature

Volume 01 : **Green** / *with an introduction by* **Philip Jodidio**

with over 200 illustrations

Contents

Paths to
Enlightenment / *Philip Jodidio*

'Architecture is about the quality of space and details,' states architect Vo Trong Nghia. 'It is a matter of the scale of spaces, of the quality of light and materials. You can't just put a tree on a building and say it's green architecture.'

Vo has undertaken a broadening palette of different projects united by his desire to bring together nature, architecture and modern materials and methods. 'We want to use vernacular and modern design together to help solve the problems of high-density cities like Ho Chi Minh and Hanoi,' he explains. 'Vernacular design really harmonizes with nature. It was already there before electricity. It knew how to deal with really hot weather, for instance. Nowadays, with higher population density and less land, vernacular design cannot be applied 100 per cent of the time. So we began to develop a new type of architecture to harmonize with these new conditions, and with modern lifestyles. I've tried to make architecture become a mini-park for the city. We've learned from the local vernacular how to use simple materials and techniques.'

Where Vo's main building material was the bamboo he first imagined using having come across a book about the Columbian architect Simón Vélez, he now sees the issues in a broader way. 'We use bamboo, timber, rammed earth, stone and more,' he says. 'We use trees not as decoration, but as an essential element of architecture.

House for Trees, Ho Chi Minh

We want trees and all natural materials to interact with the building – to limit water and flooding, to filter sunlight and sounds, to improve high-density living. On top of that, we try to recycle water and use solar panels. We try to merge natural energy and materials.'

Projects that implement these ideas include Stacking Green (2001) in Ho Chi Minh, a 65 m² (700 sq ft) house built on a narrow, 20 × 4 m (66 × 13 ft) site, with the front and back façades covered entirely with concrete planters, which are cantilevered out from two side walls. An automatic irrigation system inside the planters provides humidity. There are few partition walls to maximize both interior fluidity and views of the green walls. This vertical garden, along with the rooftop garden, helps to shield residents from street noise and pollution. Natural ventilation is provided through the walls and two top openings. Here, Vo says, 'we have adhered to the bioclimatic principles of the traditional Vietnamese courtyard house.'

Another, more recent project in the same vein is the House for Trees (2013; opposite), also in Ho Chi Minh. Built for a $156,000 budget on a 474 m² (5,100 sq ft) site, the house is divided into five 'prisms', which, as Vo explains, were designed as 'devices of greening', or ' pots' for planting trees on the rooftops. The gaps between these prisms form small gardens, allowing residents to experience the surrounding greenery throughout the house. The prisms themselves are connected by covered semi-outdoor spaces, which, along with the interior and the gardens, provide living space for the residents. This is an experimental house in a tropical climate with an ambiguous relationship between inside and out.

Although an increasingly large number of architects across the world are intensifying the use of plants in their designs, Vo takes a different approach. 'I was a farmer, and I love trees,' he says. 'I observe which ones I should use, and pick the plants myself.' This extensive use of planting allows for a reduction in the cost and complexity of cladding in Vietnam's warm climate. Vo adds: 'The trees are planted within a system that is independent from the buildings in order to simplify maintenance. When we design a building, we ask the owners if they love plants. If they do, it's easy to maintain them without much outside intervention. In Vietnam, people often take care of plants in the city as a kind of hobby.'

Referring to his rejection of the idea that simply planting trees on a building makes it green, Vo says, 'I speak frequently about building a system that connects people and nature. The building itself can be compared to an ecosystem in which people live. Being in a building should be like being in a park, or even a forest. Our office is like a monastery, an office and a resort, all at the same time. Birds and insects and animals have all come to live around our building. It became its own ecosystem, although at first it was an artificial creation.'

Nor is the work of Vo Trong Nghia circumscribed by his interest in bamboo or buildings planted with trees. His Low Cost House project prototypes (2012) in Dong Nai province measure about 20 m^2 (215 sq ft) in size and cost just $3,200 per house. The aim of the scheme was to provide homes for low-income residents in the Mekong Delta area. The plans were designed to be adjustable, allowing for future expansion for family members and functions, with residents participating in the construction to further reduce costs. A polycarbonate panel wall, corrugated FRP panel roof and bamboo louvres were the main materials used.

Although Vo has been meditating since 2012, he recently took his Buddhist faith a large step further, spending three years (2017 to 2020) at the Pa-Auk Tawya Meditation Centre. Founded in 1926, the retreat is located in a forest in the Taung Nyo Mountains in

Chicland Hotel, Da Nang

Myanmar, 15 km (9 miles) southeast of Mawlamyine. There he studied the Five Precepts, the basic code of ethics for the lay followers of Buddhism.

The Five Precepts

1. Do not harm or kill
2. Do not take what is not given
3. Do not engage in sexual misconduct
4. Do not lie or gossip
5. Do not take intoxicating substances

'The Five Precepts are part of Buddhist teaching,' Vo explains. 'There should be no lying and no stealing. So although it is not difficult to obtain pirated software in our country, we refuse to do that and buy 100 per cent of what we use. We also refuse to use Photoshop in photographs of our work, because making a building look different than it is, is a form of lying. In the office, we do not drink alcohol or smoke. Killing anything, including ants and mosquitoes, is also forbidden.'

Vo has applied these rules both to his own studio and to all of those who work on his projects. 'If we maintain those five precepts, we can have a very peaceful society,' he explains. 'When people apply to work with us, we explain that they

must accept these rules. Everyone must also meditate for two hours each day. Workers on our construction sites must also meditate for one hour each morning.'

Vo's commitment to these religious teachings is firm, and he feels he has fundamentally changed his way of working as a result of his time at the retreat. 'I spent three years in Myanmar to be enlightened,' he says. 'I believe that architecture is secondary to enlightenment. At the studio, meditation and maintaining the Five Precepts are our first priorities. While I was in Myanmar, I continued to work, but only for thirty minutes a day. The studio is doing very well, because I have a lot of free time. I work no more than two hours a day now. When you can develop what I call "super-concentration", everything becomes easy and clear.'

He adds: 'I sometimes do very simple line sketches, and then explain my idea to my colleagues. That is how I worked when I was in Myanmar. Since my employees also meditate, they understand me very well. Without meditation, our minds wander after just a few seconds and you cannot focus well on any subject. If we are able to focus, architecture becomes easier to understand. I imagine a building in my mind, as well as forty or fifty details, and then … finished!'

Binh House, Ho Chi Minh

This almost subliminal approach to architectural design is certainly surprising, but becomes even more so as Vo reveals more about his process. 'With concentration, you can overcome time and distance,' he says. 'I have not been to many of the buildings I designed. This was, of course, partly because of the three years I spent in Myanmar, but I have also developed such concentration that I don't feel that I need to visit. A client recently asked me to design another building for him – although I had already done work for him, we had never met. I start with notes that are given to me about what the client wants and about issues such as local building regulations, along with photographs of the site. I can quickly understand the context – the weather, the materials, even the nearby trees. I can even feel the humidity and the wind. I can see the activity of people. Before I began meditating, I had to think a lot more about concepts, but now I don't always have architecture in my mind.'

When asked how he would define his own success, Vo answers with a single word, 'enlightenment', adding that if he became celebrated as a famous architect, it would be meaningless in comparison. He does, however, remain a very active architect, despite his assertion that he devotes little time to the actual process of conceiving projects. His abiding desire to create

deep links between nature and architecture has resulted in many spaces that create a sense of wellbeing or, indeed, a kind of inspirational moment.

'For a building to last a long time, it has to be loved and respected by the people who use it,' Vo says. 'If users don't like a building, they want to tear it down. Sometimes I feel that my buildings are like churches or chapels, even when their purpose is not religious. There is a spiritual element. Because we meditate, the calmness of some of our work does approach the spiritual.'

Vo has travelled and designed buildings outside of Vietnam, but today his direction seems to be guided by his faith and perhaps his desire to spread the word about the Five Precepts. When asked what he does with the rest of his time if he only works for half an hour a day, he laughs and says, 'I am learning English,' before adding that meditation is one of his principal activities.

'My English was very bad and I started to learn nine months ago,' he adds. 'But I am really old, I am forty-four, so the work is slow. After studying English for another three months, I would like to go to the United States to explain the importance of the Five Precepts and meditation, perhaps in a famous university.' He laughs. 'They had a president who was always lying, and I think I can help them.'

Ha Long Villa, Ha Long

Projects

01.1_

Binh Thanh House / *Ho Chi Minh, Vietnam*

Located in the centre of Ho Chi Minh, Binh Thanh House was designed for two families: a couple in their sixties and their son, his wife and their child. The plot has a dual character, being in a typical urban area, facing onto a dusty, noisy street, but close to the river and the Saigon Zoo and Botanical Gardens, which form a backdrop of greenery.

The design also needed to accommodate the tropical climate and two different lifestyles – one natural and traditional, utilizing natural lighting and ventilation with water and greenery, and the other modern and temperate, aided by air-conditioners. The building comprises three stacked, floating volumes, wrapped by concrete blocks. Between these volumes are two spaces covered by glass but open to the outside, where residents can enjoy the sunshine, greenery, wind and water.

The three volumes are slightly offset to bring in natural light and create small gardens on each storey. The floor of each volume serves as the ceiling for the in-between spaces. Surfaces were designed with a variety of curved shapes, providing each space with different light effects. Bedrooms and other small rooms are contained within the semi-enclosed volumes to enhance security and privacy. By contrast, the open spaces in between function as independent living spaces for the two families.

The patterned blocks, which used to be a popular building material in Vietnam as a means of creating natural ventilation, are made from pre-cast concrete and measure 60 cm (24 in.) in width and 40 cm (16 in.) in height. They help shield the residents from harsh sunlight and heavy rain, as well as provide privacy. While this building looks different from other townhouses in Ho Chi Minh, the architectural solutions are derived from the local conditions and lifestyles of the residents. Modern life and nature can become compatible with one another, with the house offering an interpretation of an ecological way of living within the contemporary tropical city.

Pre-cast concrete blocks on the top-floor terrace

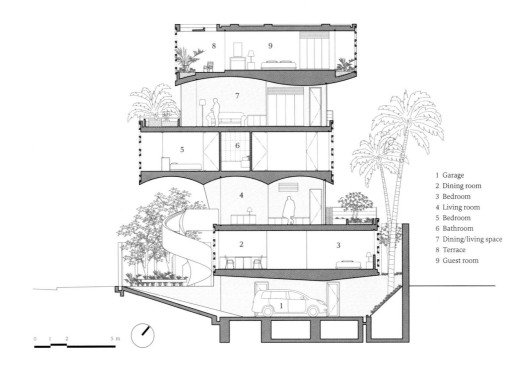

1 Garage
2 Dining room
3 Bedroom
4 Living room
5 Bedroom
6 Bathroom
7 Dining/living space
8 Terrace
9 Guest room

0 1 2   5 m

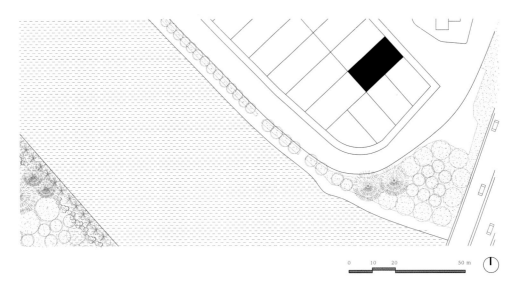

0   10   20   50 m

top *Section*
above *Site plan*
opposite *Streetside façade*

above *Terrace and bedroom on the top floor*
opposite *A concrete spiral staircase leads up to the first-floor living room*

above *The dining/living space on the third floor*
opposite *View from the top-floor bedroom out to the terrace*

above *Patterned blocks and planting provide variations in the façade*
opposite *A concrete staircase opens out to fresh air and green space*

Farming Kindergarten / *Dong Nai, Vietnam*

This kindergarten for 500 children of low-income factory workers is a prototype for sustainable educational spaces in tropical climates. The building itself was designed as a continuous ribbon, forming an interlocking clover shape, which creates three internal courtyards. The ribbon has two large openings, maximizing natural ventilation and lighting.

Vietnam has an abundance of productive land for agriculture, including the Mekong Delta. Recently, however, floods, salt damage and droughts have taken their toll. There are also serious urban concerns, such as air pollution. The country ranks among the highest with poor air quality, owing primarily to the presence of factories and abundance of motorbikes. Vietnam's cities are also losing their vegetation. Consequently, there are few safe playgrounds to play in, leading to risks of children becoming

sedentary. Our mission was to create a green kindergarten that would counteract these problems.

The architectural and mechanical energy-saving methods that were applied include, but are not limited to, a green roof, pre-cast concrete louvres for shading, recycled materials, water recycling and solar water heating. The continuous green roof has space for planting fruit and vegetables and provides a safe outdoor playground. The three courtyards seem as if drawn with a single stroke, rising and dipping down, allowing the children a very special eco-friendly experience as they walk along the roof and wander through the courtyards. The roof is also a place to teach children about the importance of agriculture and for building a relationship with nature.

Vegetable beds in the roof garden

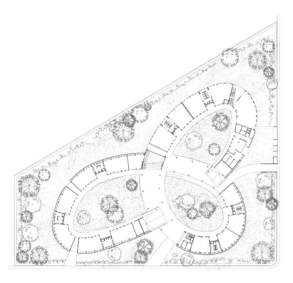
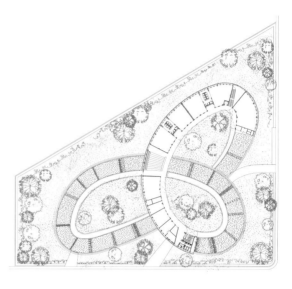

0 5 10   20 m

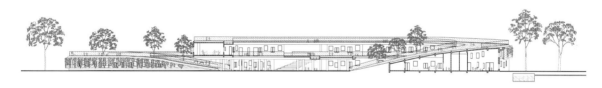

0   5   10   20 m

top *Site plans*
above *Sections*
opposite, above *Bird's-eye view of the kindergarten*
opposite, below *Class activities on the roof*

The rooftop vegetable garden is part of the children's learning experience

Windows in the ribbon maximize cross-ventilation and natural light

Pilotis support an overhanging roof, sheltering open-air spaces for play

01.3_

House for Trees / *Ho Chi Minh, Vietnam*

Vietnamese cities have experienced rapid urbanization, leaving their origins in sprawling tropical forests far behind them. In Ho Chi Minh, for example, only 0.25 per cent of the city is covered with greenery. An overabundance of motorbikes causes traffic congestion, as well as serious air pollution. As a result, recent generations of the population have lost their connection with the natural world.

House for Trees, located in the Tan Binh district of Ho Chi Minh and built with a budget of US $156,000, is an effort to change this. The aim of the project was to bring green space back into the city, and to provide residences in high-density neighbourhoods with large tropical trees. The house comprises five tower-like structures, with each topped by a concrete box that acts as a giant planter. The planters also function as storm-water basins – extending the idea to other houses in the future could potentially reduce the risk of flooding in the city.

The towers are slotted into the plot to create a central courtyard, with small gardens between. Together, these spaces become part of the ground-floor living space, with large glass doors and windows opening onto the courtyard to bring in plenty of natural light and ventilation. On the other side of the house, there are fewer windows for privacy and security. Communal areas such as the dining room and library are on the ground floor, with bedrooms and bathrooms above connected via a steel bridge.

Outside, the walls were made from in-situ concrete with bamboo formwork, while the interior walls were built using locally sourced bricks. A hollow layer separates the concrete and brick to protect the interior space from heat radiation. By using natural and locally sourced materials, we were able to reduce both cost and carbon footprint, and produce a design that blurs the boundaries between inside and out. House for Trees offers a tropical lifestyle for co-existing with nature.

View of the five rooftop 'pots' with planting

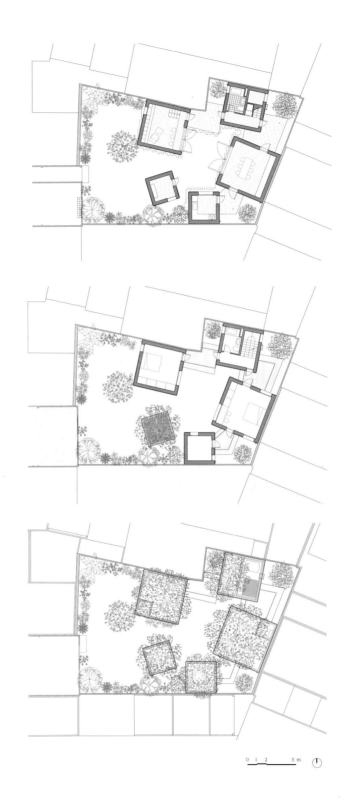

above *Floor plans*
opposite *Walls are made from in-situ concrete with bamboo formwork*

The private courtyard, with each room opening onto it

The courtyard at night

A House in Nha Trang / Nha Trang, Vietnam

This house is in the city of Nha Trang in central Vietnam, bordered by the ocean and the mountains. The client wanted a large house with outside space, so we designed the roof as a hanging garden with plenty of greenery. The local building codes, however, required nearly half the roof area to be sloped and covered in tiles. To comply with the guidelines and maximize green space, the roof was divided into parallel bands of alternating green 'tiles'. This not only gives residents the opportunity to live in nature, but also to improve the local area, with the various species of plants enriching the ecosystem.

Nha Trang House is part of the House for Trees project, with designs replicated under the same concept but adapted for each site condition. The area is particularly scenic, but it is also a developing residential neighbourhood in danger of losing its identity. We designed a house that would resonate with its splendid surroundings, responding to the building codes in a way that would not be superficial or stereotypical.

The large, single roof with its many trees departs from the scale of a private house, and is more like infrastructure or a public park that is open to the neighbours. In their sheltered and shady garden, the residents can enjoy the views against a backdrop of plants.

In developing countries such as Vietnam, low-tech building methods are still dominant, without the aid of advanced technology. The structure of the project, therefore, comprises a reinforced concrete frame with brick walls – the most common and economical building method in Vietnam. The brick wall contains a hollow void between its two layers, which serves as insulation to reduce heat radiation and to make the building more watertight. Finally, the walls have been painted white, inside and out. Overall, the design is an economic but aesthetically pleasing and sophisticated solution.

The rooftop greenery connects the house to its surroundings

Abundant planting fills the rooftop garden

0   1   2   5 m

above *Sections*

opposite *The inner courtyard, separating the living and dining spaces*

above *The bedroom, looking out to the outer courtyard*
opposite *The dining room at night*

above *The zig-zag roof terrace*
opposite *The interior courtyard*

The Babylon / *Da Nang, Vietnam*

Located on the main road between Da Nang and Hoi An old town is the Naman Retreat (see also *Bamboo*, vol. 2, pp. 134–59), a coastal resort in Ngu Hanh Son district, 16 km (10 miles) from Da Nang International Airport. The retreat caters to the physical and mental wellbeing of guests through immersion in nature and activities such as yoga and beach sports, all in a friendly environment. To help guests achieve the ideal atmosphere for the purification and relaxation of mind and body, the complex was designed as a harmonious mix of greenery, stone and bamboo.

The first phase of the project was the development of a 3.4-hectare site between the road and the beach, with three types of accommodation – beach villas, bungalows and hotel – set within the lush, green landscape. The hotel, The Babylon, is clad in pre-cast concrete louvres, with planting climbing up them to provide both privacy and visual separation from the road, and help to minimize thermal radiation during the

hot season in this tropical climate. The formwork gives the concrete a wooden texture that is in keeping with the hotel's natural surroundings.

Inside, the thirty-two rooms are arranged across three floors in an L-shape around the swimming pool. The pool is visible from the balconies above, which are partially shielded behind the green façade. There is planting in every corner of the resort, and arriving at The Babylon feels like diving into a tropical landscape. The façade of greenery comprises a combination of trees and vines, including *Quisqualis indica* (Rangoon creeper, or Chinese honeysuckle), while *Vernonia elliptica*, *Spathiphyllum wallisii* (peace lily) and *Aglaia duperreana* appear along the corridors and balconies. Together, they create a diverse vertical landscape.

Vertical louvres with planting cover the exterior

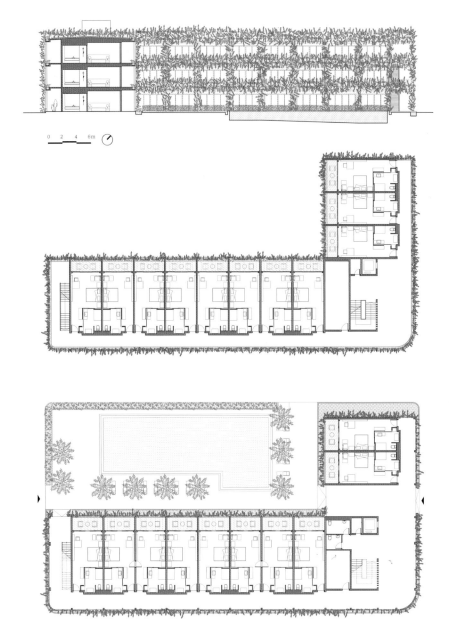

0 2 4 6m

above *The green façade*
opposite, above *Elevation*
opposite, below *Typical floor plans*

Planting climbs up the vertical louvres and provides shade

View from the entrance to the pool and restaurant

One of the guest-room balconies, overlooking the pool

01.6_

Binh House / *Ho Chi Minh, Vietnam*

Another project in the House for Trees series, Binh House was designed to provide the residents with green space within a high-density neighbourhood. Living in the house are three generations of one family, so the challenge was to create spaces that allow family members to connect and communicate.

Gardens were placed on top of the vertically stacked spaces, accessed by sliding-glass doors, which improves the microclimate by allowing fresh air and daylight into each room. The offset openings also increase visibility and interaction among the family. Living and dining spaces, bedrooms and studies are continuously open, with sightlines from each room reaching beyond to the other spaces via the gardens.

Service areas such as the kitchen, bathrooms, stairs and corridors are located at the west side of the house to limit heat-radiation exposure in frequently used areas. The vertical variation of spaces creates a lopsided pressure difference, so that when the neighbouring houses are built, ventilation will be maintained. Thanks to these passive strategies, the house will remain cool in the tropical heat.

In the rooftop garden, large trees provide shade, reducing the interior temperature, and there is room for growing vegetables. This vertical farming solution is both suitable for high-density housing and helps to maintain the Vietnamese way of life. By using sustainable materials such as natural stone, wood and exposed concrete, the maintenance and day-to-day costs of running the house are greatly reduced. The design not only meets functional and aesthetic concerns, but also offers a means of connecting people to people, and people to nature.

Exterior view of the house

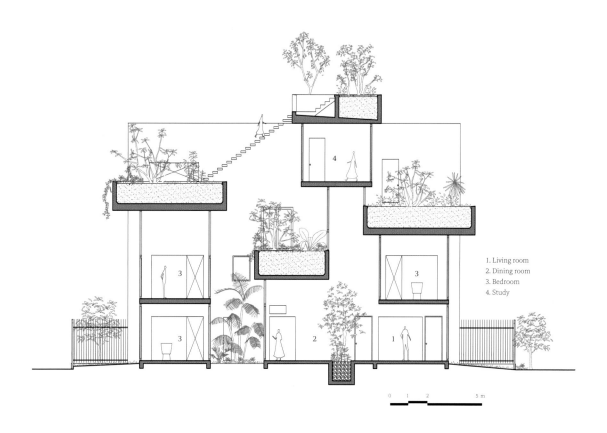

1. Living room
2. Dining room
3. Bedroom
4. Study

0 1 2   5 m

above *Section*
opposite *The double-height dining/living space*

View from the rooftop garden into the study

The first-floor bedroom, looking to the inner courtyard

above *Filtered sunlight illuminates the outdoor bath*
opposite *The double-height bathroom, filled with natural light*

above *The garden between the dining and living spaces*
opposite *Binh House at night*

01.7_

Atlas Hotel Hoian / *Hoi An, Vietnam*

The Atlas Hotel Hoian is located in the city's old town, an area that has experienced rapid growth since being designated a UNESCO World Heritage Site in 1999. Many of its ancient houses have been converted into shops and restaurants, catering for the daily influx of tourists. The traditional tiled roofscapes and internal courtyards have been slowly disappearing owing to chaotic commercial flow. As a consequence, Hoi An's old town has lost some of the peace and tranquility it was known for.

Because the hotel site was on an irregular plot of land, the design approach was to turn this constraint into a defining characteristic. We divided the linear layout into several internal courtyards. By lifting the building above the site to leave the ground floor completely free for an interconnected network of courtyards, it created a spatial quality that both reflected the dynamism of the new Hoi An and retained the charm of its historic old town.

The five-storey hotel comprises forty-eight guest rooms, a restaurant, café, rooftop bar, spa, gym and swimming pool.

Owing to the complexity of the site, each guest room is shorter and wider than in a typical hotel, but we saw this as an opportunity to give guests greater access to greenery from the bedrooms and bathrooms. The building is clad in locally sourced sandstone, used in combination with an exposed concrete slab and a series of planters along the corridors. The planters line the entire façade of the hotel, providing shade from the sun and allowing cooling breezes into the interior spaces, reducing the need for air-conditioning. Perforated stone walls also help daylight to enter the building without blocking air flow.

The use of these natural elements embodies the focus of our practice and the House for Trees concept: to integrate greenery into design as a way of rejuvenating urban areas and contributing to societal improvement. At its core, Atlas Hotel Hoian represents the reconnection of people with nature.

View of the pool, surrounded by greenery

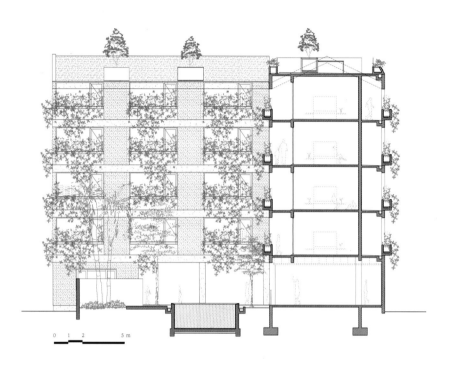

0 1 2   5 m

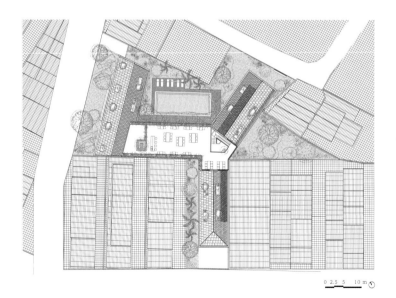

0 2.5 5   10 m

top *Section*
above *Site plan*
opposite Chrysanthemum indicum *spills over the concrete planters*

The ground-floor restaurant, with a view of the pool

The pool at night

Stepping Park House */ Ho Chi Minh, Vietnam*

The site for this design, one of the latest projects in the House for Trees series, is located in a new residential area of Ho Chi Minh, with a park along its northern edge. It is a rare opportunity to get a site in the city that is adjacent to a green public space, so we focused on creating a house that would become an extension of its surroundings by integrating the greenery of the park into the inside space.

The aim of the design was to create the feeling of being in a forest, despite being indoors. We started by creating a large void by cutting diagonally through the volume of the three floors of the house. On the ground floor, this void serves as a living room, open to the park, and on the top floor as a green-covered family room, with shade provided by louvres. It incorporates circulation and planting, and provides bedrooms and other private rooms – situated in solid volumes – with additional light. Planting trees in the opening of these volumes blocks direct sunlight, allows cool air to flow through and brightens up the interior space with green.

Opening the void diagonally to bring in natural ventilation produces a chimney effect, and reduces the need for air-conditioning. Residents walking through the space will feel the breeze flowing from the living room to the top floor of the house. Outside, the façade is covered in ivy, which also helps to ease the intense sunshine of Vietnam's tropical climate.

The shortage of green space throughout the country is behind such environmental issues as urban flooding, overheating and air pollution. Presenting a solution to these problems is an urgent challenge that architecture must address. To do so, we integrate planting into our designs as much as possible, even in small houses, creating pockets of parkland in the city. Our aim is for the 'green building' concept to spread across the world.

Streetside view of the house

top *Elevation*
above *Section*
opposite *View of the house from the park*

above *The planting continues across the three floors*
opposite *Interior private spaces*

View of the house from above

The top-floor terrace

Ha House / Ho Chi Minh, Vietnam

This private home for a family of three generations, another project in the House for Trees series, is located in an emerging residential area, a fifteen-minute drive from the centre of Ho Chi Minh. The houses in the development are terraced, and the site was very narrow, at 7 m (23 ft) wide by 20 m (66 ft) long. For this kind of typical, high-density development in South East Asia, we proposed a housing strategy that would be suitable for the tropical climate, where residents and nature could exist together.

The clients' first request was a large garden, where the children could play and the adults could entertain, along with a swimming pool, room to exercise and a bedroom for the grandmother, and a living room, kitchen/diner and sufficient space for parking – all on the ground floor. We divided the garden into smaller, connected outdoor spaces. As the building volume climbs up from the ground floor, it is gradually set back, before cantilevering out 2 m (6 ft) at the top. The stepped gardens are entwined with the terrace, continuing up to the top floor. Trees provide shade, filter sunlight and cool the air before it enters the house, with each tree acting as a screen from the main road.

The terraces on each floor vary in size, according to function. In some places, they form private gardens that can be accessed directly from the bedrooms. In others, the terrace becomes a communal garden where the entire family gathers. These individual outdoor gardens together form a single, continuous space, entered by the residents via the steel staircase outside.

Inside, the ground and first floors are connected by a central void, which connects the living room, kitchen/diner, library and children's bedrooms to become one huge space. Elongated sites like this can often be narrow, so we created large openings of different scales and proportions throughout the house. The gaps created by the shifting volumes allow in light and fresh air. As direct sunlight is reduced by the planting on the façade of the house, electricity usage will also be decreased.

Because of the tight budget, we had to keep the final costs as low as possible. We applied bricks as a finishing material, a method commonly used in construction sites in Vietnam that also reduces overall construction cost. Labour costs were kept to a minimum, and we were able to control the quality of the bricklaying on site. Since brick is a local material, the carbon footprint caused by transportation was also reduced. As with the other houses in the House for Trees series, we aim to not just plant trees in houses, but also to create a new type of dwelling in which the lives of the residents and nature become more closely intertwined.

Looking down from the rooftop terrace

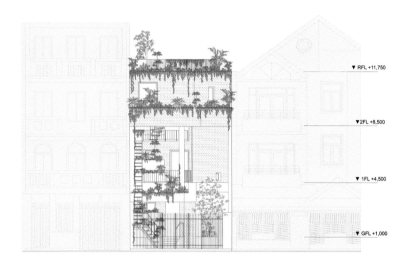

▼ RFL +11,750

▼2FL +8,500

▼ 1FL +4,500

▼ GFL +1,000

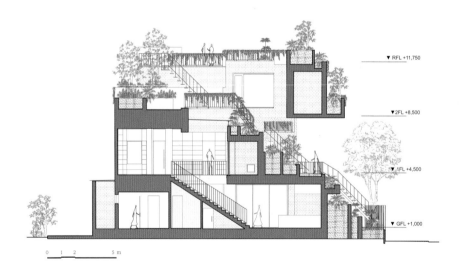

▼ RFL +11,750

▼2FL +8,500

▼ 1FL +4,500

▼ GFL +1,000

0 1 2   5 m

top *Elevation*
above *Section*
opposite *View from the street*

above *A bedroom on the first floor*
opposite *Light infiltrates the space via a triangular skylight*

View from the bedroom to the library

The dining space on the ground floor

above   *The spa on the top floor*
opposite   *Skylight above the staircase*

Chicland Hotel / *Da Nang, Vietnam*

My Khe Beach in Da Nang is a popular tourist destination in Vietnam and, according to *Forbes* magazine, one of the most charming beaches in the world. The metropolitan areas of South East Asia, and particularly Vietnam, are growing rapidly, resulting in urban forests of concrete tower blocks. Da Nang is no exception, and its many real-estate developments have disrupted the natural beauty of the Vietnamese coastline.

Our design for the Chicland Hotel, which faces directly onto the beach, about 100 m (328 ft) from the shore, set out to create an iconic structure filled with as much greenery as possible on a small site of only 700 m² (7,535 sq ft), and to be an exemplar for other tropical cities like Ho Chi Minh, Jakarta or Bangkok. We wanted to both meet the business requirements of the client, but also to not be confined by the dictates and expectations of commercial architecture.

The hotel's façade features vertically stacked concrete planters on each floor, with sky gardens and green balconies for every room. Da Nang experiences strong sunlight and heavy rainfall throughout the year, so creating a living wall for a high-rise building on the beach posed a challenge, and the position and level of each balcony had to be carefully studied to determine the best plants to use. The planting system also created a microclimate, acting as the 'lung' for the building. Inside, the space benefits from filtered air and diffused light, reducing unwanted solar heat. Because the double-skin façade casts deep shadows, the building conserves energy consumption through passive cooling. The façade also complements the interior design, as the furniture and finishes are made from local and natural materials, such as wood, stone, bamboo and rattan.

The hotel has a total floor area of 10,500 m² (113,021 sq ft), comprising 153 rooms across twenty-one storeys, with a café and restaurant, and a spa and sky bar with infinity pool on the rooftop. All of the rooms have generous views, whether out to sea or of the surrounding landscape. The exterior walls are made from concrete, designed for ease of maintenance while minimizing water penetration, making the building highly sustainable over a longer period of time.

The green façade, seen from the street

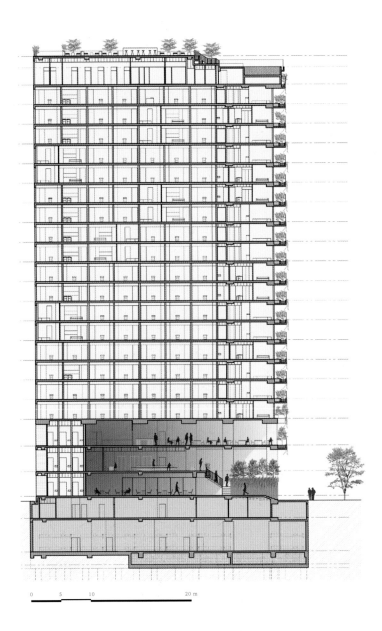

0   5   10   20 m

above *Section*
opposite *View of the dramatic façade of the hotel*

The design of the lobby area makes use of local materials

Bamboo was used for the walls and ceiling in the café

A corner guest room with terrace

Another of the hotel's guest suites

Breathing House / *Ho Chi Minh, Vietnam*

Located in the heart of Ho Chi Minh, Breathing House is a single-family home on a 4 m (13 ft)-wide, 18 m (59 ft)-deep plot, which is only accessible via a tiny alley. In this extremely dense urban setting, we wanted to design a house that would introduce an outside environment, while also ensuring privacy.

Owing to the small size of the site, the opening up of the house was confined to the front, top and back. We wrapped these three surfaces with a 'green veil' made from creeper plants, grown on a steel mesh. Planter boxes were attached with modular galvanized steel elements at each floor level to create a soft layer that acts as an environmental diffuser, filtering direct sunlight and reducing exposure while also offering a feeling of protection for the residents.

Inside the veil, the building comprises five connected tower-like volumes. The external spaces, or 'micro-voids', created by the staggered arrangement of the volumes provide multiple indirect lighting and ventilation routes throughout the house. In this narrow, deep plot, flanked by neighbours on both sides, it was more environmentally effective to get ventilation into each corner of the building via multiple voids, rather than through a single large courtyard.

The micro-voids have openings on each floor, through which residents have views from every point in the house. The staircase was also designed as a micro-void, with light coming in from above and openings into the rooms. The building's porous composition favours natural ventilation over air-conditioning, creating spatial and visual connections throughout the house. The significance of the project is that it created a green space in the heart of a crowded, growing mega-city, and we hope that the essence of the design will be a positive influence on other cities of Vietnam, which is losing its green spaces at an alarming rate.

Light penetrates into the space via the green veil

above *Bird's-eye view of the heavily planted rooftop*
opposite *Streetside view*

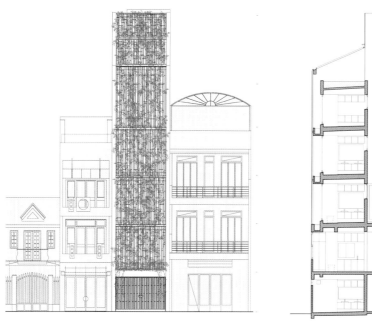

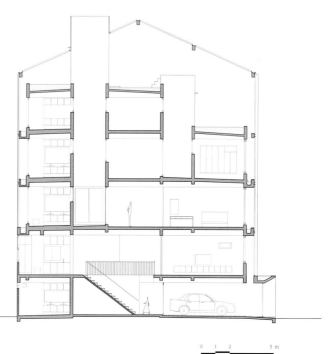

above, left   *Street elevation*

above, right   *Section*

opposite   *The micro-void continues from the terrace to the roof*

View to the outside through the vertically planted louvres

above *Living room*
opposite *View from the street at night*

01.12_

Thang House / *Da Nang, Vietnam*

Inspired by childhood visions of a country house full of tropical plants, the client wanted a similar home for himself and his family. Located in the heart of Da Nang, the site was very small – around 250 m² (2,691 sq ft) – so we devised a design strategy that would create a green 'lung' for the house by dividing the land into two parallel sections: one for the garden, with a huge green wall alongside it, and the other for the living space. The majority of the windows and doors face this 'lung', so that natural light, fresh air and the scent of grass and flowers penetrate every corner of the house.

Any green area that was lost owing to construction work was compensated by the introduction of a rooftop garden, which gets sunlight and shelters the building. The garden includes nine tree boxes, interspersed with gaps so that the planting is visible by day and by night. This has not only contributed to the greening of the city, but has also created a space for the family to grow their own fruit and vegetables. This combination of gardening with a panoramic view provides the ideal antidote to the burden of city life.

The aim was to make the house self-sufficient in food production and to minimize energy consumption. To help it operate more sustainably and economically, an automatic watering system recycles and circulates water from the fish pond to the roof garden, while solar water-heating and a solar panel system on the roof produce enough energy for a family-sized home. Inside, the house comprises four boxes: one large volume beneath the roof, and three smaller volumes inside it, which overhang the garden to allow space for bedrooms and a living room.

Building materials were sourced from nearby, including grey stone from Hoa Son mine and white brick from Quang Nam province. The largest box is covered in stone, with the smaller boxes clad in brick, giving the living spaces a light and friendly feel. The narrow roof gaps allow sunshine to subtly penetrate the interior space, creating the effect of light playing through the void across three levels. The exposed concrete is also an efficient low-tech construction material, and stands up to the harsh local climate.

Thang House is part of the House for Trees series, which aims to improve the urban landscape through sustainable and environmentally friendly architecture. The lack of greenery in Vietnamese cities has created a variety of problems, from increased pollution to rainwater retention, as well as leading to inactivity in people over time. Our design seeks to address these problems by creating a tranquil space for each member of the family, while also preserving a green corner in the middle of this rapidly changing city.

View from the entrance to the pool

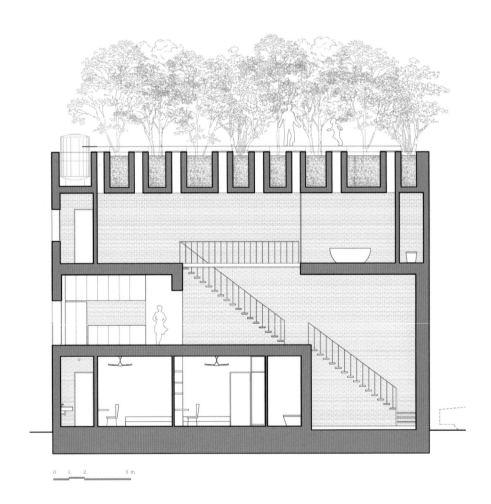

0   1   2   5 m

above *Section*
opposite *View to the terrace*

above *Looking up from the living space to the dining area on the terrace*
opposite *View down to the pool and out to the street*

View from the pool up to the living/dining space (left) and bedroom (right)

above *View from the terrace to the master bedroom*
opposite *Natural light filters into the master bedroom*

View out to the bathroom and terrace from the master bedroom

01.13_

Viettel Academy
Educational Centre / *Hanoi, Vietnam*

Viettel Academy Educational Centre is part of a training facility run by Viettel, a global telecommunications group with offices in cities across Vietnam, including Hanoi, Ho Chi Minh and Da Nang, and over 27,000 staff (as of 2015). Its central position within Hoa Lac Hi-Tech Park, some 30 km (19 miles) from Hanoi, makes it easily accessible from the residential zone and other facilities in the campus.

The aim of the design was to provide short-term accommodation and educational space that would be quiet and peaceful, allowing trainees to concentrate on their studies away from the hustle and bustle of city life. The twelve buildings comprise classrooms, meeting rooms, halls and offices – with the main blocks four to five storeys high, and the rest two to three storeys high – and surrounded by an overflow pool, which helps to regulate the centre's cooling microclimate. The blocks are connected by multi-level circulation paths, including corridors, ramps and staircases, offering views and quiet places for study.

Hanoi's humid tropical climate led to the design of a lightweight concrete roof, which shelters the majority of the semi-outdoor spaces. It also functions as a skywalk and helps reduce direct exposure to sunlight. Planting is interspersed between the blocks, creating a friendly atmosphere for trainees, while a series of roof gardens on the different floors provides further space for relaxation and socializing.

Locally produced bricks were used to create the impressive monolithic red-brick façade, 30 to 40 cm (12 to 16 in.) thick, which comprises two layers of bricks with a void between for insulation and to reduce energy use. This brick façade forms a warm backdrop to the students' activities, with the combination of red brick and green plants creating a harmonious atmosphere for the centre.

View of the red bricks of the building façade

0   5   10   20 m

0   5   10   20 m

above *View of the centre*
opposite, above *Site plan*
opposite, below *Floor plan*

above *Elevated pathway between the blocks*
opposite *View down to the pathway and pool*

Natural light filters down deep into the interior spaces

Viettel Offsite Studio / *Hanoi, Vietnam*

Viettel Offsite Studio, along with the Viettel Academy Educational Centre's campus (pp. 164–75), is also part of Viettel's training campus at Hoa Lac Hi-Tech Park, near Hanoi. Positioned at a corner of the site, the studio complex sits in a quiet lakeside setting on a slight slope with abundant trees, and comprises six units: a reception area, a dining space and four studios.

The arrangement of the six V-shaped blocks follows the landscape. Connected by an open corridor, the blocks are triangular, with one side open to views of the lake and trees.

The walls have been built high intentionally to block strong sunlight from the east and west, with small openings that allow in filtered light and gentle breezes to the rooftop studio and garden.

Together, the monumental walls of the V-shaped blocks create an impressive façade. Opening out from the interior space to the outdoors, the walls form an 'open book', allowing staff members to relax, focus the mind and be immersed in nature.

View of the blocks and pathway from the courtyards

above *View of the hallway*
opposite, above *Elevation*
opposite, below *Site plan*

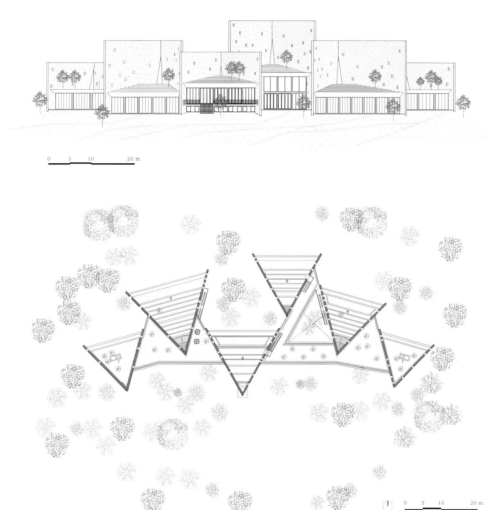

Looking out to the triangular courtyard and lake

above *View from the rooftop garden*
opposite *Holes cut into the wall allow light and air flow*

Ha Long Villa / *Ha Long, Vietnam*

Vietnam's economic growth, thanks to the increase in tourism, has raised the country's standard of living, but it has also led to the reckless development and destruction of natural sites. To address this situation, we designed a house that would reconnect people to nature. Ha Long Villa, the latest in the House for Trees series, is located in Ha Long, a coastal city with many local industries, including fishing and coal mining, 160 km (99 miles) northeast of Hanoi. It is also home to Ha Long Bay, a UNESCO World Heritage Site, and is a rapidly developing tourist destination.

The design features a pentagon within a pentagon, with layers of interior and semi-exterior spaces filled with planting. This buffer zone between inside and out creates deep shadows and protects the house from the heat and noise. Each semi-exterior space is connected by the main spiral staircase, which itself creates a spatial sequence from the ground floor to the roof, lined with large windows and planting to allow views of the natural landscape and city to be experienced from different angles. It also connects the living area with the terrace, with space for gardening and relaxing. These distinctive zones offer residents different dining to entertaining options from day to day.

The exterior walls are made from rough exposed concrete, which gives the impression they have been made from stone found in nearby Ha Long Bay. The planting in the semi-exterior spaces casts shadows across this strong façade, creating an ever-changing appearance. The contrast between the rough concrete and soft vegetation – along with the dozens of plants on the roof, suggesting an area that is several times larger than it actually is – creates a vivid and lasting impression.

The open staircase provides views of the city

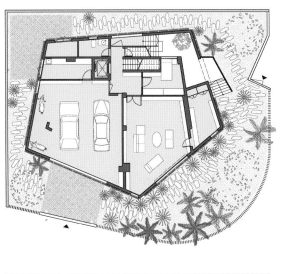

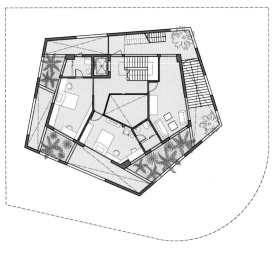

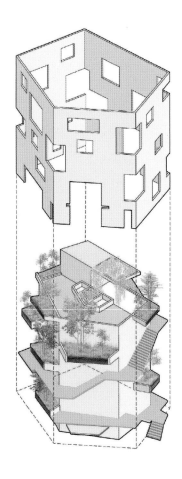

0 1 2   5 m

above *View of the street from the stairwell*
opposite, left *Floor plans*
opposite, right *The exterior shell and circulation route*

The dining area

above *View from one of the bedrooms to the outside*
opposite *Ha Long Bay, glimpsed through the trees and the concrete shell*

01.16_

Bat Trang House / *Bat Trang, Vietnam*

Bat Trang House is situated in a village in the Gia Lam district of Hanoi. The brief was to design a home for a family of seven, which could also function as a place where relatives could gather together, and as a shop, selling the traditional ceramic wares of the village. Outside, the façade of the house pays tribute to the ceramics-producing culture of the local area, while inside are the conveniences and comforts of modern life. The layout was based on the client's ideal home, with nature intertwined with the other functions of the house.

Because of the region's rich cultural heritage, and because the owner is also a ceramics specialist, the use of local materials was a priority. Pottery has its own rough aesthetic and is highly durable, so it was suitable for the outside skin of the building, which is made entirely from ceramic bricks. The bricks were made individually to size and create an alternating rhythm of open and closed spaces, with the gaps acting as vents, allowing the air to circulate throughout the building. Plants were placed in the larger openings of the façade so that light can filter through.

The design of the interior spaces took a minimalistic approach. Large glass panels were used without fear of the house becoming overheated, as direct sunlight is filtered by the layers of bricks and planting. The gaps in the walls are especially effective in achieving the right amount of solar gain, particularly in the summer. There is no need for air-conditioning, as the ventilation system of alternating bricks and green spaces, along with the doorway, ensures that the house remains cool, and provides constantly changing views for the residents. Solar panels and rainwater collectors are also part of the sustainable design.

The intimate connection between people and nature was an important part of the design for the house. We make sure that a natural and sustainable quality of living is present in every project. Here, our design allows residents to feel the ambient sunlight and freshness of the greenery as they go about their daily lives.

View from the living room down to the street level

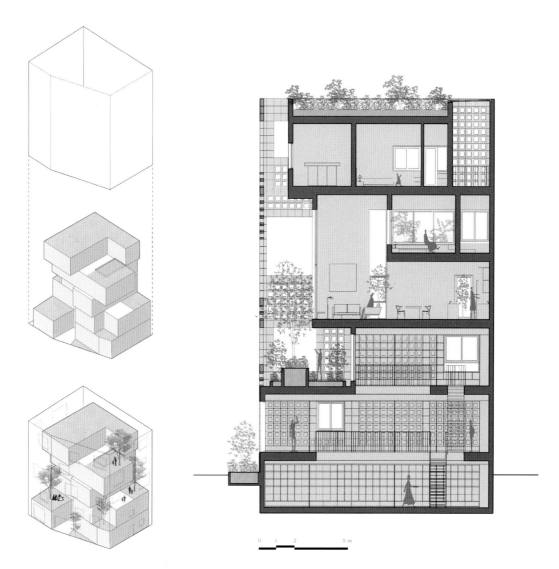

0   1   2   5 m

above, left *Diagrams*
above, right *Section*
opposite *Side perspective*

Ceramic bricks and planting form a permeable barrier between inside and out

above *The living/dining space*
opposite *View from the entrance to the living area above*

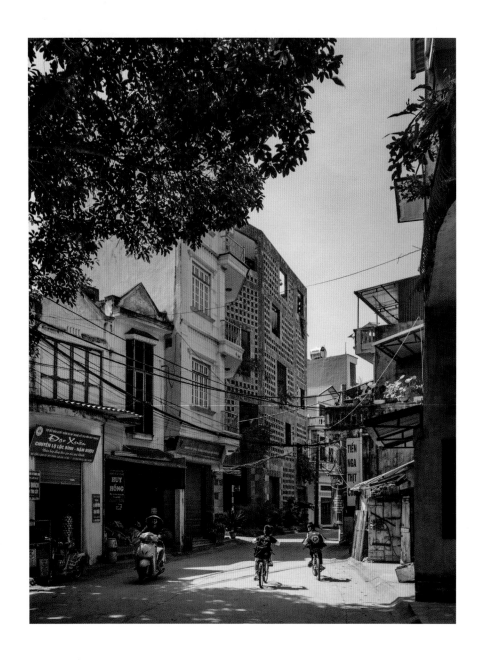

above *Street perspective*
opposite *Elevation*

Project credits

01.1 Binh Thanh House / pp. 24–35

Location: Ho Chi Minh, Vietnam
Completed: 2013
Design: VTN Architects (Vo Trong Nghia Architects)
Collaborator: Sanuki + Nishizawa Architects
Lead architects: Vo Trong Nghia, Shunri Nishizawa,
    Daisuke Sanuki
Architects: Le Thi Anh Huyen, Nguyen Tuan Anh
Programme: Residential
Gross floor area: 516 m² (5,554 sq ft)
Site area: 140 m² (1,507 sq ft)
Client: Individual
Contractors: Wind & Water House JSC,
    Danang Company

01.2 Farming Kindergarten / pp. 36–45

Location: Dong Nai, Vietnam
Completed: 2013
Design: VTN Architects (Vo Trong Nghia Architects)
Lead architects: Vo Trong Nghia, Takashi Niwa,
    Masaaki Iwamoto
Architects: Tran Thi Hang, Kuniko Onishi
Programme: Education
Gross floor area: 3,800 m² (40,903 sq ft)
Site area: 10,650 m² (114,636 sq ft)
Client: Pou Chen Vietnam
Contractor: Wind and Water House JSC
Green building consultant: Melissa Merryweather
CFD analysis: Environment Simulation, Inc.

01.3 House for Trees / pp. 46–55

Location: Ho Chi Minh, Vietnam
Completed: 2014
Design: VTN Architects (Vo Trong Nghia Architects)
Lead architects: Vo Trong Nghia, Masaaki Iwamoto,
    Kosuke Nishijima
Architect: Nguyen Tat Dat
Programme: Residential
Gross floor area: 226 m² (2,433 sq ft)
Site area: 474 m² (5,102 sq ft)
Contractor: Wind and Water House JSC

01.4 A House in Nha Trang / pp. 56–67

Location: Nha Trang, Vietnam
Completed: 2015
Design: VTN Architects (Vo Trong Nghia Architects)
Collaborator: ICADA (icada.asia)
Lead architects: Vo Trong Nghia, Masaaki Iwamoto
Programme: Residential
Gross floor area: 277 m² (2,982 sq ft)
Site area: 492 m² (5,296 sq ft)

01.5 The Babylon / pp. 68–79

Location: Naman Retreat, Da Nang, Vietnam
Completed: 2015
Design: VTN Architects (Vo Trong Nghia Architects)
Lead architect: Vo Trong Nghia
Design management: Takashi Niwa
Design team: Nguyen Viet Hung
Masterplan for Naman Retreat Resort: VTN Architects
    (Vo Trong Nghia Architects)
Programme: Hospitality
Gross floor area: 2,480 m² (26,695 sq ft)
Site area: 1,517 m² (16,329 sq ft)
Client: Thanh Do Investment Development &
    Construction JSC
Contractor: Thanh Quan JSC
namanretreat.com

01.6 Binh House / pp. 80–91

Location: Ho Chi Minh, Vietnam
Completed: 2016
Design: VTN Architects (Vo Trong Nghia Architects)
Lead architect: Vo Trong Nghia
Design team: Masaaki Iwamoto, Chiang Hsing-O,
    Nguyen Tat Dat, Nguyen Duy Phuoc, Takahito Yamada
Programme: Residential
Gross floor area: 233 m² (2,508 sq ft)
Site area: 322 m² (3,466 sq ft)
Contractor: Wind & Water House JSC

01.7 Atlas Hotel Hoian / pp. 92–101

Location: Hoi An, Vietnam
Completed: 2016
Design: VTN Architects (Vo Trong Nghia Architects)
Interior design: VTN Architects (Vo Trong Nghia
    Architects)
Lead architects: Vo Trong Nghia, Tran Thi Hang
Design team: Le Thanh Tung, Pham Huu Hoang,
    Pham Khac Hung, Nguyen Thi Ha Vi, Le Thanh Tan,
    Nguyen Ngoc Thien Chuong
Programme: Hotel and leisure
Site area: 1,348 m² (14,510 sq ft)
Gross floor area: 3,115 m² (33,530 sq ft)
Client: DANH Co., Ltd
atlashoian.com

01.8 Stepping Park House / pp. 102–13

Location: Ho Chi Minh, Vietnam
Completed: 2018
Design: VTN Architects (Vo Trong Nghia Architects)
Lead architects: Vo Trong Nghia, Hidetoshi Sawa
Project architect: Nguyen Van Thien
Programme: Residential
Site area: 252 m² (2,713 sq ft)
Gross floor area: 475 m² (5,113 sq ft)
Contractor: Wind and Water House JSC

01.9 Ha House / pp. 114–23

Location: Ho Chi Minh, Vietnam
Completed: 2019
Design: VTN Architects (Vo Trong Nghia Architects)
Lead architects: Vo Trong Nghia, Tran Thi Hang
Design team: Takahito Yamada, Le Viet Minh Quoc,
    Mitsuyoshi Shingu
Programme: Residential
Site area: 137 m² (1,475 sq ft)
Gross floor area: 175 m² (1,884 sq ft)
Contractor: Wind and Water House JSC

01.10 Chicland Hotel / pp. 124–37

Location: Da Nang, Vietnam
Date: Under construction
Design: VTN Architects (Vo Trong Nghia Architects)
Lead architects: Vo Trong Nghia, Takashi Niwa
Design team: Ngo Thuy Duong, Mai Lan Chi,
    Nguyen Van An
Interior design: VTN Architects
    (Vo Trong Nghia Architects)
Programme: Hospitality
Site area: 699 m² (7,524 sq ft)
Gross floor area: 10,495 m² (112,967 sq ft)
Client: CHIC-LAND JSCo.
Main contractor: Hicon
Mechanical and electrical engineers: NDC
    Consulting JSCo.
Civil and structural engineers: SMT Viet Nam JSCo.

01.11 Breathing House / pp. 138–47

Location: Ho Chi Minh, Vietnam
Completed: 2019
Design: VTN Architects (Vo Trong Nghia Architects)
Lead architects: Vo Trong Nghia, Kosuke Nishijima
Project architect: So Adachi
Programme: Residential
Site area: 69.5 m² (748 sq ft)
Gross floor area: 343 m² (3,692 sq ft)
Contractor: Wind and Water House JSC

01.12 Thang House / pp. 148–63

Location: Da Nang, Vietnam
Completed: 2019
Design: VTN architects (Vo Trong Nghia Architects)
Lead architect: Vo Trong Nghia
Design team: Le Phuong Uyen, Kosuke Nishijima
Programme: Residential
Site area: 250 m² (2,691 sq ft)
Contractor: Thang

**01.13 Viettel Academy
        Educational Centre** / pp. 164–75

Location: Hanoi, Vietnam
Completed: 2019
Design: VTN Architects (Vo Trong Nghia Architects)
Lead architect: Vo Trong Nghia
Design team: Ngo Thuy Duong, Do Minh Thai,
    Do Huu Tam
Programme: Education
Gross floor area: 2,651 m² (28,535 sq ft)
Site area: 9,026 m² (97,155 sq ft)
Client: Viettel Corporation
Contractor: Delta Corp

01.14 Viettel Offsite Studio / pp. 176–89

Location: Hanoi, Vietnam
Completed: 2019
Design: VTN Architects (Vo Trong Nghia Architects)
Lead architect: Vo Trong Nghia
Design team: Marek Obtulovic, Nguyen Van Thu
Supervision: Nguyen Hoang Son, Đoan Huu Chính
Programme: Office
Gross floor area: 1,427 m² (15,360 sq ft)
Client: Viettel Corporation
Contractor: Delta Corp

01.15 Ha Long Villa / pp. 190–205

Location: Ha Long, Vietnam
Completed: 2020
Design: VTN Architects (Vo Trong Nghia Architects)
Lead architect: Vo Trong Nghia
Design team: Nguyen Van Thu
Programme: Residential
Site area: 514 m² (5,533 sq ft)
Gross floor area: 1,190 m² (12,809 sq ft)

01.16 Bat Trang House / pp. 206–17

Location: Bat Trang, Vietnam
Completed: 2020
Design: VTN Architects (Vo Trong Nghia Architects)
Lead architect: Vo Trong Nghia
Design team: Ngo Thuy Duong, Nguyen Van An,
    Do Huu Tam, Pham Phuong Thao
Programme: Residential
Site area: 220 m² (2,368 sq ft)
Gross floor area: 740 m² (7,965 sq ft)

Photo credits

All plans and drawings provided courtesy of
VTN Architects (Vo Trong Nghia Architects)

All photographs by Hiroyuki Oki,
apart from the following:

17 Ha Tien Anh; **37** Quang Tran;
38 (top) Gremsy (flyingcam.com.vn);
38 (bottom) Quang Tran; **40** Quang Tran;
126–7 Ha Tien Anh; **129** Ha Tien Anh;
136–7 Ha Tien Anh

Index

Page numbers in *italics* refer to illustrations

Thanks to Koji Yamamoto, Quang Tuan Ta and Vu Tran Huy Phi for their editorial assistance, and to Le Hien and Nguyen Hoang Tri Nhan for content editing. And special thanks to all of the staff at VTN Architects for their contribution to this book.

Vo Trong Nghia studied architecture at the Nagoya Institute of Technology and the University of Tokyo, before founding Vo Trong Nghia Architects in 2006 in Ho Chi Minh, Vietnam. His designs are at the foregront of 'green' architecture and sustainable practices, and have recieved numerous accolades, including multiple World Architecture Community Awards and a *Wallpaper** Design Award in 2021.

Philip Jodidio studied art history and economics at Harvard, and edited *Connaissance des Arts* for over twenty years. His books for Thames & Hudson include *Casa Tropical: Houses by Jacobsen Arquitetura* and *The New Pavilions*.

First published in the United Kingdom in 2022 by
Thames & Hudson Ltd, 181A High Holborn, London WC1V 7QX

First published in the United States of America in 2022 by
Thames & Hudson Inc., 500 Fifth Avenue, New York, New York 10110

Vo Trong Nghia / Building Nature – Volume 1: Green
© 2022 Thames & Hudson Ltd, London
Text © 2022 Vo Trong Nghia Architects
Introduction © 2022 Philip Jodidio

Designed by Steve Russell / www.aka-designaholic.com

British Library Cataloguing-in-Publication Data
A catalogue record for this book is available from the British Library

Library of Congress Control Number 2021942696

ISBN 978-0-500-34359-3

Printed in China by RR Donnelley

Be the first to know about our new releases, exclusive content and author events by visiting
thamesandhudson.com
thamesandhudsonusa.com
thamesandhudson.com.au

On the cover:
Front *Chicland Hotel, Da Nang (Photo: Ha Tien Anh);*
Back *Binh House, Ho Chi Minh (Photo: Hiroyuki Oki)*

On the slipcase:
Front *Huong An Vien Welcoming House, Hue (Photo: Hiroyuki Oki)*
Back *Ha Long Villa, Ha Long (Photo: Hiroyuki Oki)*

On pp. 2–3: *The Babylon, Da Nang*
pp. 4–5 *Viettel Academy Educational Centre, Hanoi*
pp. 6–7 *Viettel Offsite Studio, Hanoi*
p. 10 *Thang House, Da Nang*
pp. 12–13 *Ha Long Villa, Ha Long*